The SOLAR SYSTEM, METEORS and COMETS

First published in 2015 by Wayland
© Wayland 2015

Wayland
Hachette Children's Books
338 Euston Road
London NW1 3BH

Wayland Australia
Level 17/207 Kent Street
Sydney, NSW 2000

Produced by White-Thomson Publishing Ltd.

White-Thomson Publishing Ltd
www.wtpub.co.uk
+44 (0) 843 208 7460

All rights reserved.

Editor: Izzi Howell
Designer: Clare Nicholas
Cover design and concept: Lisa Peacock

A catalogue for this title is available from the British Library

ISBN: 978 0 7502 9231 3

eBook ISBN: 978 0 7502 9232 0

Dewey Number: 523.2-dc23

10 9 8 7 6 5 4 3 2 1

MIX
Paper from
responsible sources
FSC® C104740

Wayland is a division of Hachette Children's Books,
an Hachette UK company.

www.hachette.co.uk

CONTENTS

MEET THE NEIGHBOURS

Earth is not alone. It exists in a star system called the solar system along with seven other planets, more than 160 moons and many other smaller bodies. Formed around five thousand million years ago, the solar system is so big that it would take a passenger airliner flying at over 900 km/h 17 years to travel to Earth from the Sun.

Centre Of Attention

At the centre of the solar system lies a 1,390,000-km-wide star – the Sun. Made almost entirely of hydrogen (71%) and helium (27%) gases, and dwarfing all of its neighbours, the Sun contains more than 99% of all the matter found in the solar system.

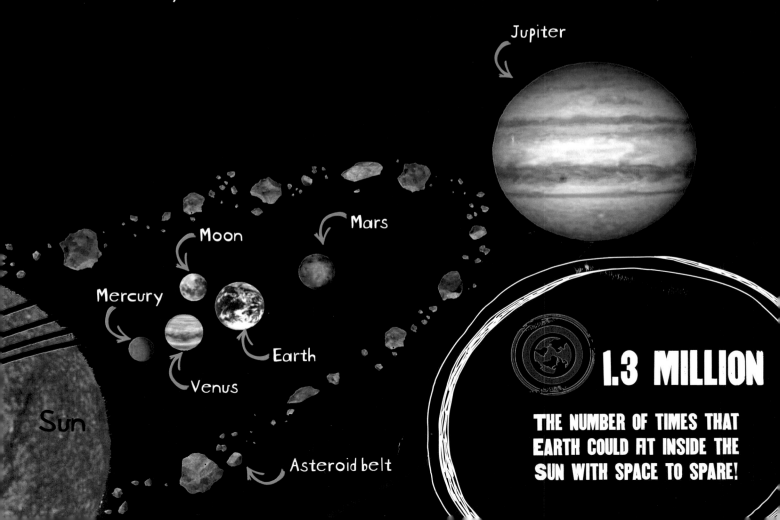

Jupiter

Moon

Mars

Mercury

Earth

Venus

Sun

Asteroid belt

1.3 MILLION

THE NUMBER OF TIMES THAT EARTH COULD FIT INSIDE THE SUN WITH SPACE TO SPARE!

Inner And Outer

The eight planets that orbit the Sun can be divided into the four inner planets, which are mainly rocky, and the four outer planets, which are much larger and made mostly of gas. Between these two groups lies a broad belt of smaller bodies, made of rock and metal, called asteroids.

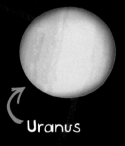

Neptune

Uranus

Saturn

IS NEPTUNE THE END OF THE SOLAR SYSTEM?

Beyond Neptune's orbit, and stretching out as far as 50-55 AU from the Sun, lies a cold, mostly empty region of the solar system known as the Kuiper Belt. It contains asteroids, Pluto and a number of other dwarf planets.

ASTRONOMICAL DISTANCES

Because distances in the solar system are so huge, scientists use special units of measurement. An Astronomical Unit (AU) is the average distance between Earth and the Sun – 149,597,871 km. Mercury is just 0.38 AU from the Sun whilst Neptune is 30.1 AU away.

SOLAR FURNACE

In the Sun's core, a massive nuclear furnace rages with temperatures as high as 15 million °C. The Sun uses up a staggering 600 million tonnes of hydrogen gas every second, fusing the nuclei (centre) of hydrogen atoms together to form helium atoms. These nuclear-fusion reactions generate vast amounts of energy.

WHAT'S A PLANET; WHAT'S A MOON?

Sun (star)

Earth (planet)

Moon

You may be standing still, but the planet you're on is whizzing through space at 107,200 km/h! Planets are spherical bodies that travel on a long path around a star. This path is called an orbit. Moons have orbits too, but they move around planets, not stars.

Can You Feel The Force?

Gravity is an invisible yet powerful force of attraction between objects. All objects exert gravity, but the greater an object's mass (the amount of matter it contains), the greater its gravitational pull. The Sun's mass is so high that it draws the planets into orbit around it. The time it takes a planet to complete a full orbit of the Sun is called a year.

OVAL ORBITS

A planet's path through space is not a perfect circle, but an ellipse (oval). This means that a planet's distance from the Sun changes throughout its orbit. The furthest point from the Sun is known as the aphelion. The point when the planet is nearest the Sun is called the perihelion.

Spinning Through Space

As they travel along their orbital path, planets and moons also move in another way, spinning on their axis. A complete 360° turn is known as a rotational period or day. Saturn's day is under 11 hours long whilst slow-spinning Venus's day lasts 5,832 hours!

Amazing Moons

Not all moons in the solar system are like Earth's Moon. Neptune's largest moon, Triton, has massive, deep canyons and ice volcanoes which blast out clouds of methane and nitrogen gas. One of Jupiter's moons, Europa, is covered in ice, below which there may be a giant underground sea.

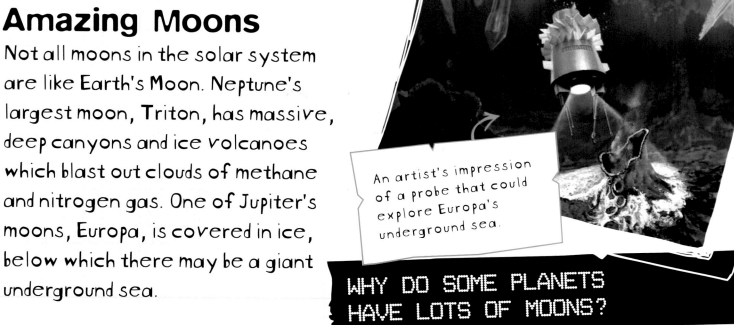

An artist's impression of a probe that could explore Europa's underground sea.

WHY DO SOME PLANETS HAVE LOTS OF MOONS?

The bigger the planet, the greater its gravity. This means that the gravity of larger planets stretches further into space and captures more objects. Jupiter and Saturn, the two biggest planets, have more than 60 moons each, whilst the smallest planet, Mercury, has none.

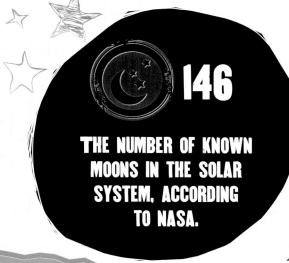

146

THE NUMBER OF KNOWN MOONS IN THE SOLAR SYSTEM, ACCORDING TO NASA.

NO-GO IO

Jupiter's closest moon, Io, is also the solar system's most volcanically active body. Over 400 erupting volcanoes emit clouds of sulphur up to 500 km high and spout out more than 100 times the lava of all the volcanoes on Earth.

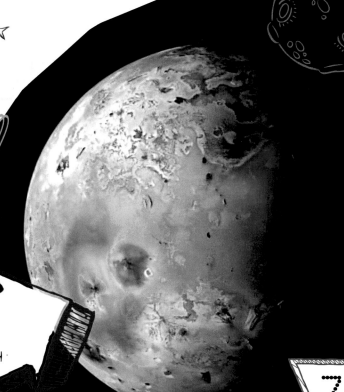

The dark spots on Io mark areas of volcanic activity.

PLANET EARTH

The only known planet that supports life, Earth was formed around 4.6 billion years ago. Dust, ice and rock orbiting the infant Sun clumped together and grew in heat and size. The planet cooled, the atmosphere formed and life began.

Vital Statistics

Earth is the fifth-largest planet in the solar system and the biggest of the four rocky planets. It has a 12,756-km diameter through its equator – the imaginary line around its middle.

About 70% of the Earth's surface is covered by water, of which around 97% is salt water. Most of the fresh water on the planet is locked into the frozen ice caps found at the North and South poles.

mantle

crust

inner core

outer core

EARTH'S COMPOSITION

Earth's inner core is made of solid iron and nickel, surrounded by a molten iron and nickel outer core. Covering the core is a 2,900-km-thick rocky mantle. This is largely solid, but it can bend and distort. On top of the mantle is a thin, brittle crust, which measures 30–50 km thick on land but only 5–15 km on the ocean bed.

IT'S A GAS!

Earth's atmosphere is crucial to supporting life, as it both blocks out harmful radiation from space and keeps the planet warm. The atmosphere is composed of 77% nitrogen, 21% oxygen, 1% water vapour and trace elements of gases such as argon and carbon dioxide.

ice cap

At An Angle

Earth is tilted at an angle of 23.5° relative to the Sun. It is this tilt which creates the seasons. Summer occurs in the hemisphere (half) of the planet that is more tilted towards the Sun, allowing the Sun's rays to pass through less of Earth's atmosphere and strike a more concentrated part of the Earth's surface.

1.5 MILLION

THE NUMBER OF DIFFERENT SPECIES OF LIVING THINGS CATALOGUED BY SCIENTISTS ON EARTH SO FAR. THE TOTAL NUMBER MAY BE MORE THAN EIGHT MILLION.

Northern hemisphere spring/Southern hemisphere autumn

Northern hemisphere winter/Southern hemisphere summer

Northern hemisphere summer/Southern hemisphere winter

Northern hemisphere autumn/Southern hemisphere spring

THE MOON AND ITS ORBIT

Formed around 4.5 billion years ago when a large object crashed into Earth, the Moon is a rocky, crater-marked body. It orbits at an average distance of 384,400 km from Earth – equal to nine trips around Earth's equator.

Lunar Landscape

The Moon's surface is strewn with rocky craters created millions of years ago by meteorites and asteroids. The largest craters are more than 400 km wide. Meteorites still strike the Moon's surface. In 2013, a 40-cm-wide meteorite travelling at 90,000 km/h hit the lunar surface, creating an impact equal to exploding 4,000 kg of dynamite!

DOES THE MOON HAVE GRAVITY?

The Moon only exerts one-sixth of the gravity you find on Earth. Whilst Earth's gravity keeps the Moon in its orbit, the Moon's gravity pulls on Earth as well. It causes bulges in the world's water, which move as Earth rotates to form tides.

MARIA AND MOUNTAINS

Maria are large rocky plains, covered by a layer of rubble and dust 5–10 m deep. They make up almost one-sixth of the Moon's surface. The Moon also has mountains, the tallest of which, Mons Huygens, rises 5,500 m above the surrounding area.

10

Face To Phase

The Moon completes an orbit of Earth in 27.32 Earth days – the same amount of time it takes to complete one spin on its axis. This is known as a synchronous orbit and means that the same side of the Moon always faces Earth. A phase of the Moon is the amount of it lit by the Sun that we can see from Earth. This gradually changes from a thin crescent to a full Moon in a cycle lasting 29 days.

Astronauts left behind food pouches, used towels and bags of their urine. Yuck!

LUNAR LITTER
Lunar missions have left behind a lot of rubbish including broken-down lunar vehicles, crashed space probes, a set of space boots and a golden olive branch (a sign of peace).

Footprint Fact
The Moon has very little atmosphere and no winds or water to wipe out marks made on its surface. This means that the footprints made by the 12 astronauts who stepped on the Moon during the Apollo missions (1969-1972) are still there.

382
THE AMOUNT OF ROCK IN KILOGRAMS COLLECTED FROM THE MOON BY ASTRONAUTS DURING THE APOLLO MISSIONS, FOR ANALYSIS ON EARTH.

MERCURY AND VENUS: STRANGE NEIGHBOURS

The two planets nearest the Sun – Mercury and Venus – are both named after ancient Roman gods. Neither has moons, but they are different in many ways.

Mini Mercury

The smallest planet, with a diameter of 4,879 km, Mercury is also the densest. Mercury's surface has been battered by meteorite and asteroid impacts, which have left behind cliffs over 1000 m tall and dozens of craters. Because the planet has next-to-no atmosphere, there are no winds or rain to erode these features. Many are over 3.8 billion years old.

Can you see the smiling face in Mercury's suitably named Happy Little Crater?

LONG DAYS, SHORT YEARS

Mercury takes just 88 Earth days to complete its orbit around the Sun, moving at serious speed – about 170,000 km/h. However, the Sun's gravity puts the brakes on Mercury's rotation, making its days very long. The Sun only rises on Mercury once every 176 days!

No planet has a bigger temperature swing than Mercury, which can be as cold as -180 ºC or as hot as a thermometer-busting 430 ºC.

Earth's Twin?

At 12,104 km in diameter, Venus is a similar size to Earth and is our nearest neighbour. More than 20 space probes have been sent to explore the planet but found that the similarities with Earth ran out quickly. Venus lacks water on its surface and its heavy atmosphere presses down with 90 times more force than Earth's atmosphere. Thick layers of clouds rain down drops of sulphuric acid.

Sapas Mons

HOW LONG IS A DAY ON VENUS?

As crazy as it sounds, Venus's day (243 Earth days) is longer than its year (224.7 Earth days).

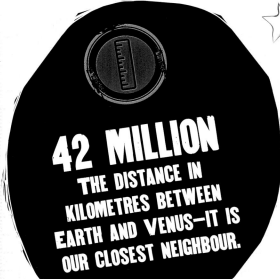

42 MILLION
THE DISTANCE IN KILOMETRES BETWEEN EARTH AND VENUS—IT IS OUR CLOSEST NEIGHBOUR.

VERY STRANGE VENUS

Venus is a hostile place, with its thick, carbon-dioxide-rich atmosphere, which acts like a blanket, keeping the heat in. The surface of Venus is a sweltering 464 °C – hot enough to melt lead. At least 2,000 volcanoes can be found on the planet's surface, including Sapas Mons, a shield volcano 217 km wide – the distance between London and Cardiff.

MARS: THE RED PLANET

Mars has fascinated people for thousands of years. The Chinese called it the Fire Star and the Ancient Egyptians named it *Her Desher*, which means the Red One.

Meet Mars

Mars is the fourth planet from the Sun, lying an average distance of 227.9 million kilometres away. The planet is about half the size of Earth, with a diameter of 6,780 km . It has around 38% of the gravity of Earth, meaning that you could jump almost three times as high on Mars.

The length of a day on the red planet is similar to Earth, 24 hours and 37 minutes, but its year is longer. Mars takes 687 days to complete an orbit around the Sun.

Olympus Mons is the tallest mountain in the entire solar system. It is three times as high as Mount Everest.

WHY IS MARS RED?

Much of Mars is covered by a thick layer of soil containing a large amount of iron-based minerals. The red that you can see is actually rust – iron oxide – formed millions of years ago.

MOONS AND MOUNTAINS

Mars has two tiny moons, discovered in 1877 by Asaph Hall and named Phobos and Deimos. Looking rather like giant potatoes, these two rocks may actually be asteroids captured by Mars's gravity. The largest of the two, Phobos, is just 26.8 km across.

Mars Missions

More than 45 spacecraft have either orbited Mars or landed on its surface. The first successful lander was Viking 1 in 1976. The Curiosity Rover has been trundling around the planet since 2011!

Both the European Space Agency (ESA) and the National Aeronautics and Space Administration (NASA) have targets to send people to Mars by 2040!

The car-sized Curiosity Rover snaps a selfie on Mars after making a 563,000,000-km journey from Earth.

Life On Mars?

There's no life on Mars today, but some scientists believe that liquid water once ran across the planet's surface and it may have harboured some form of life in the distant past.

TO CAP IT ALL ...

Mars has a thin atmosphere, made up mostly of carbon dioxide. Temperatures on the planet range from a balmy 25 °C to a freezing cold -125 °C. At its two poles, Mars has ice caps made of frozen water and carbon dioxide.

4,000

THE LENGTH IN KILOMETRES OF THE ENORMOUS VALLES MARINERIS CANYON SYSTEM ON MARS. IF PLACED ON EARTH, THE 200-KM-WIDE, 7-KM-DEEP CANYON WOULD STRETCH ACROSS THE ENTIRE UNITED STATES.

JUPITER: IT'S MASSIVE

The Juno mission is due to reach Jupiter in 2016, and will carry out experiments to help us understand the origin and evolution of the planet.

The biggest planet in the solar system, Jupiter is so large that 1,300 Earth-sized planets could fit inside it. Jupiter has almost two and a half times the mass of all the other planets combined. In other words, it's massive!

Its Place In Space

Jupiter lies an average of 778 million km from the Sun – about 5.2 times further from it than Earth. It takes Jupiter 11.86 Earth years to complete an orbit around the Sun, travelling at a speed of just over 47,000 km/h. From Earth, it's the third-brightest object in the night sky, after the Moon and Venus.

HOW MANY MOONS DOES JUPITER HAVE?

Jupiter has more moons than any other planet. There are 67 known Jovian moons, four of which (Io, Callisto, Ganymede and Europa) were first spotted by Italian astronomer, Galileo, as far back as 1610.

UNDER PRESSURE

Jupiter is known as a gas giant and its gases, mostly hydrogen and helium, get thicker and denser the closer to the centre of the planet you go. At depths of 14,000 km or more, massive pressure turns the gases into liquid metal. This gives Jupiter a huge magnetic field that stretches out almost as far as Saturn.

Stunning Stripes

The planet's distinctive stripes are caused by different areas of its atmosphere rising and falling. The lighter, rising, bands are called zones and the darker, sinking, regions are called belts. The belts contain molecules made of hydrogen, oxygen and carbon. The zones contain clouds of frozen ammonia crystals that reflect sunlight.

zone

belt

The Great Red Spot is big enough to contain two or three Earth-sized planets.

Speedy Spinner

Despite being huge, Jupiter is no slouch. It's the fastest-spinning planet in the solar system, taking only 9 hours, 56 minutes and 30 seconds to complete a full turn on its axis. This rapid rotation gives the planet a bulging waistline at its equator, as well as flattened north and south poles.

SPOT THE STORM

In 1665, the Italian astronomer Gian Cassini described a feature on Jupiter's surface that we now call the Great Red Spot. It turned out to be an enormous storm, about 25,000 km by 12,000 km in size. The storm is still raging today, with 500 km/h winds that make hurricanes on Earth look puny!

142,984
THE DIAMETER IN KILOMETRES OF JUPITER – ABOUT 11 TIMES LARGER THAN EARTH.

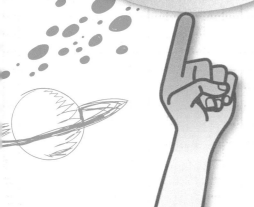

SATURN: LORD OF THE RINGS

The sixth planet from the Sun, Saturn is the furthest planet that can be seen from Earth without a telescope. It's famous for its stunning rings and many, many moons.

What A Whopper!

With a diameter of 120,536 km, Saturn is the second-largest planet in the solar system. Despite its giant size, it spins on its axis rapidly. A day on Saturn lasts just 10 hours and 39 minutes, although its year is a lot longer than Earth's. Saturn's journey around the Sun takes more than 29 years to complete.

HOW MANY MOONS DOES SATURN HAVE?

Christian Huygens was just 26 years old in 1655 when, using a home-made telescope, he became the first person to discover a moon orbiting Saturn. Since the discovery of Titan, a further 61 moons have been found.

IT'S A GAS

You couldn't stand on Saturn. Its outer layers are made of gas – mostly hydrogen, with small amounts of helium and even smaller amounts of other gases including ammonia and methane. Astronomers think that Saturn might have a rocky, icy core, about 12,000 km wide – the distance from London to Hawaii.

Because most of Saturn is lightweight gas, it's the least dense planet in the solar system, and less dense than water. This means that it would, in theory, float in a giant bath!

Ringleader

Of the four planets with rings round them, Saturn's are undoubtedly the biggest and brightest. The rings aren't solid discs – they're actually made of separate pieces of ice, dust and rock held together by gravity. Although the rings span thousands of kilometres across, in places they're only a kilometre thick.

MIGHTY TITAN

Titan is Saturn's largest moon. With a diameter of 5,150 km, it's actually bigger than the planet Mercury. Titan's surface contains lakes of liquid methane and its thick atmosphere is made up of several poisonous gases.

Scientists believe that the rings are the remains of comets, asteroids or broken-up moons.

URANUS AND NEPTUNE

These two icy giants are far away – Uranus lies an average distance of 2.87 billion km from the Sun, whilst Neptune is about 4.5 billion km away. Both planets receive very little energy from the Sun, so they are seriously cold!

Uranus Or George's Star?

Uranus was discovered in 1781 by the British astronomer William Herschel, who tried to name it after King George III. It was eventually named after the ancient Greek god of the sky. Around 60 Earths would fit inside the 51,118-km-diameter planet, which has 11 faint rings around it. A day on Uranus lasts about 17 hours, but a year is much longer as Uranus takes 84 years to orbit the Sun.

WHY IS URANUS ON ITS SIDE?

All the planets are tilted a little on their axis but Uranus's tilt is 98°, meaning the planet orbits the Sun on its side. Many astronomers believe that a really big object once struck the planet, causing its dramatic slant.

42

THE LENGTH IN YEARS OF SUMMER AT URANUS'S NORTH POLE. URANUS'S UNUSUAL SEASONS ARE DUE TO ITS TILT.

Mighty Methane

The eighth and farthest planet from the Sun, Neptune was observed by Galileo as far back as 1612. At 49,532 km in diameter, it's slightly smaller than Uranus, and looks blue due to the methane in its atmosphere. Scientists believe that both Neptune and Uranus have a small rocky core, about the size of the Earth, surrounded by thick layers of gas.

Miranda, the smallest of Neptune's 27 moons, has an unusual bumpy surface, shown here in this image taken by Voyager 2.

STORMY WEATHER

Voyager 2 is the only spacecraft so far to get up close and personal with Neptune. When it whizzed past in 1989, only 3,000 km from the planet's north pole, it discovered a mighty storm, named the Great Dark Spot. The storm was about the size of Earth and, with winds whistling around at 2,100 km/h, the fastest in the solar system.

Forget celebrating your birthday on Neptune. The planet takes a staggering 164.8 years – over 60,000 days – to complete an orbit of the Sun.

ASTEROIDS AND DWARF PLANETS

The planets are not the only bodies in the solar system to orbit the Sun. Others include dwarf planets and asteroids made of rock, metal and ice.

Belt Up

Most asteroids are found in a huge ring called the Main Belt, which lies between the orbits of Mars and Jupiter. Asteroids are believed to be the remains of a planet or moon that never fully formed. The Main Belt is largely empty space, as most asteroids are less than 1 km wide. Only 23 asteroids in the Main Belt are more than 200 km in diameter.

150

THE NUMBER OF ASTEROIDS DISCOVERED THAT HAVE MINI MOONS ORBITING THEM. SCIENTISTS THINK THERE MAY BE MANY MORE.

ASTEROID ALERT

Some asteroids are quite near to Earth and may cross Earth's orbital path. These are known as Near Earth Asteroids (NEAs) and are tracked by space agencies in case any look set to get dangerously close. In 2014, a 370-m-long NEA called 2014 HQ124 travelled 'close' to Earth – about 3.25 times the distance between Earth and the Moon.

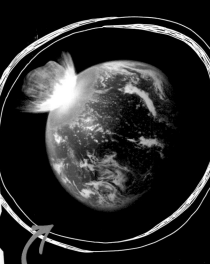

A massive asteroid impact in Yucatán, Mexico 65 million years ago, is believed to have caused the extinction of dinosaurs.

Poor Old Pluto

Discovered by Clyde Tombaugh in 1930, Pluto reigned supreme for 76 years as the smallest planet in the solar system. But in 2006, it received a downgrade, becoming a dwarf planet. Pluto is extremely distant – between 4.4 and 7.4 billion km away from the Sun. It takes 248 years to complete its orbit.

An artist's impression of Pluto with its largest moon, Charon, and two of its smaller satellites.

DWARF PLANETS

Dwarf planets aren't moons because they orbit the Sun, not a planet. They are big enough for gravity to have pulled them into round shapes, but not big enough for gravity to clear their orbital path of rocks or ice. The dwarf planet Ceres is found in the asteroid belt, while Eris and Pluto lie on the outskirts of the solar system, beyond Neptune.

WHO NAMED PLUTO?

An 11-year-old schoolgirl, Venetia Burney, suggested naming Pluto after the Roman god of the underworld. Her grandfather passed the idea on to his astronomer friends, and it was accepted!

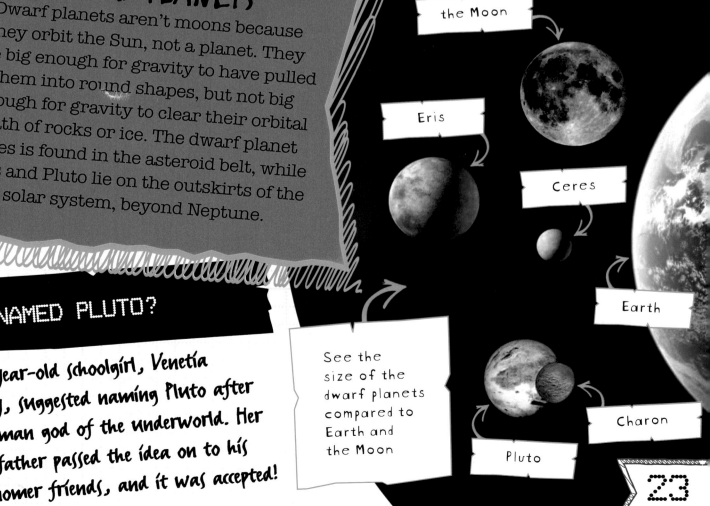

the Moon

Eris

Ceres

Earth

Charon

Pluto

See the size of the dwarf planets compared to Earth and the Moon

METEORS AND METEORITES

Earth is under attack from space! Around 100 tonnes of material hurtles towards our planet every day. Amongst this space debris are meteoroids, which may burn up in Earth's atmosphere or fall to the ground as meteorites.

Rock 'n' Metal

Meteoroids are pieces of rock or metal that travel through space, drawn towards Earth by the planet's gravity. Many are fragments of asteroids but some are debris from comets, the Moon or Mars.

Over 100 meteors can be seen every hour in the Geminids meteor shower, which happens each year in mid-December.

TAKE A SHOWER

Most meteoroids burn up in the atmosphere in seconds. These are called meteors. Some meteors melt and form streaks of light in the night sky, known as shooting stars. A collection of meteors all at the same time is known as a meteor shower.

HOW FAST DO METEORS TRAVEL?

The fastest meteors enter Earth's atmosphere at a speed of 259,200 km/h.

Impact!

Meteoroids that fall to Earth are called meteorites. Some larger meteorites create a crater on impact. Meteor Crater in Arizona, USA was formed around 50,000 years ago. A 50-m-wide meteorite crashing into the ground at a speed of more than 45,000 km/h created this 170-m-deep, 1.2-km-wide impact crater.

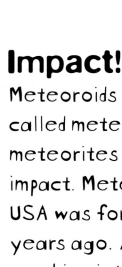

Meteor Crater

60,000
THE WEIGHT IN KILOGRAMS OF THE HEAVIEST METEORITE EVER FOUND ON EARTH, KNOWN AS THE HOBA METEORITE.

Bruising Encounter

Ann Elizabeth Hodges is the only person proven to have been struck by a meteorite. A 4-kg rock from space crashed through her roof in Alabama, USA in 1954 and bruised her left hand and hip.

COMETS

Comets are chunks of rock, dust and ice that travel through space like large, dirty snowballs, between a few hundred metres and 40 km in size. Comets come from the outer reaches of the solar system.

Burning Up

All comets orbit the Sun but most remain so far from Earth that we cannot see them. However, the orbit of some comets brings them in towards the inner planets. There, energy from the Sun heats the comet up, turning its ice to gas. This forms a hazy head, or coma, around the nucleus of the comet.

A LONG TAIL

Tails also form behind a comet – one containing dust and one containing gas. These can trail a long way behind the nucleus. The tail of Comet Hyakutake has been measured as 570 million km long – that's almost the distance between Earth and Jupiter!

gas tail

dust tail

coma

Comet Hyakutake was discovered in 1996 by an amateur astronomer in Japan, using only a pair of binoculars!

Comet Hale-Bopp was visible to the naked eye from Earth between 1996 and 1997.

Hairy Stars

Comets have been observed in the night sky for centuries and got their name from the ancient Greek for 'hairy stars'. The most famous comet of all is Halley's Comet, named after Edmond Halley who calculated that it reappeared in the night sky every 76 years.

Halley's Comet is shown in the Bayeux Tapestry, created in the 11th century.

COMET HUNTER

American Carolyn Shoemaker only took up astronomy when she was 51 but she has made up for lost time, discovering 32 comets and more than 300 asteroids! One of the comets she co-discovered, Shoemaker-Levy 9, crashed into Jupiter in 1994 at a speed of over 200,000 km/h.

250,000
THE ESTIMATED LENGTH IN YEARS OF COMET WEST'S ORBIT. DON'T WAIT UP!

Comet West was strikingly visible from Earth in 1976.

HOW LONG DOES A COMET'S ORBIT LAST?

Some comets have short orbits lasting less than 20 years, which means they become a regular feature in the night sky. Long-period comets take more than 200 years to complete an orbit, so if you've seen them once, you won't see them again!

EXOPLANETS

The solar system is not the only place in the universe where planets are found. Astronomers have always suspected that there might be planets orbiting stars other than the Sun, but they didn't have proof until the 1990s.

Needle In A Haystack

Trying to find exoplanets in the vastness of space is hard. The planets are huge distances away from Earth and are usually outshone by the stars they orbit. Planet hunters use a range of techniques to find exoplanets, including trying to spot the slight dimming of light from a star when a planet travels in front of it.

ULTIMATE EXOPLANET FINDER

The Kepler Telescope is the ultimate exoplanet hunter. Between its launch in 2009 and the middle of 2014, it helped discover a staggering 977 exoplanets. These include Kepler-16b, the first known exoplanet to orbit not one but two stars, and Kepler-70b, a planet that whizzes around its star in less than six hours!

Like something out of a sci-fi film, two suns set over the horizon of Kepler-16b.

Peculiar Planets

There are some strange exoplanets out there, including GJ 504b which is a young, bright-pink planet, and HD 209458b, which takes just 3.3 days to orbit its star. Winds of over 5,000 km/h race through the atmosphere of HD 189733b , an exoplanet that contains high levels of silica – the material from which glass is made. Some scientists have speculated that the planet may experience glass raining down on its surface.

WILL WE EVER FIND ANOTHER EARTH?

One day, astronomers hope to find a rocky world with a thick, oxygen-rich atmosphere and surface water. Sound familiar? The search mainly focuses on something called a habitable zone, where an exoplanet orbits its star at the right distance to provide enough heat to support life without being too hot.

Glass And Diamonds

If you think glass rain is nuts, another exoplanet, 55 Cancri e, is largely composed of carbon, which may have turned into diamond under enormous pressure!

2,200

THE SURFACE TEMPERATURE IN DEGREES CELSIUS OF EXOPLANET WASP-12B – HOT ENOUGH TO MELT STEEL!

GLOSSARY

axis – an imaginary line that goes through the centre of an object that is spinning

billion – a thousand million

body – an object in space

density – a measure of how much matter an object contains in its volume. If something is very dense, then it contains a lot of matter in a small space.

diameter – the distance across the middle of a circle or through the middle of a sphere

mass – the amount of matter an object contains

matter – physical things that exist in space as solids, liquids or gases

molecule – the smallest unit of a substance, containing one or more atoms

molten – rock or metal that has turned into liquid, due to heat

nucleus – the centre of an object or an atom

orbit – to travel round another object in space, usually in an elliptical path

radiation – invisible energy from heat or light

satellite – an object that moves around another object in space

spherical – something that has the shape of a sphere (a 3D circle)

tilt – to have one side higher than the other

FURTHER INFORMATION

Books

**Space Travel Guides: Earth and the Inner Planets/
  The Outer Planets**
by Giles Sparrow (Franklin Watts, 2013)

The Earth and Space: Comets, Asteroids and Meteors
by Steve Parker (Wayland, 2009)

The World in Infographics: Space
by Jon Richards and Ed Simkins (Wayland, 2013)

Websites

https://solarsystem.nasa.gov/planets
The latest news and top-quality images of space.

http://science.nationalgeographic.com/science/
space/solar-system
An excellent guide to the solar system.

http://www.bbc.co.uk/science/space/solarsystem
Information and videos about our solar system
and its planets.

INDEX

Stargazing
Optical Telescopes
Observatories
Seeing Other Waves
Radio Astronomy
Observatories in Space
Lift Off!
Space Probes
Landers and Rovers
Spacemen and Women
Astronaut Training
The International Space Station
Life in Space

978 0 7502 9228 3

Meet the Neighbours
What's a Planet, What's a Moon?
Planet Earth
The Moon and its Orbit
Mercury and Venus: Strange Neighbours
Mars: the Red Planet
Jupiter: it's Massive
Saturn: Lord of the Rings
Uranus and Neptune
Asteroids and Dwarf Planets
Meteors and Meteorites
Comets
Exoplanets

978 0 7502 9231 3

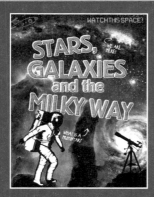

Starry Skies
Our Nearest Star
A Protostar is Born
Main Sequence Stars
Seeing Stars
Star Quality
Strange Stars
Star Death
Supernova!
Neutron Stars and Pulsars
Galaxies
Galaxy Types
The Milky Way

978 0 7502 9225 2

What is the Universe?
Investigating the Universe
How the Universe Began
Development and Formation
The Expanding Universe
Groups, Clusters and Superclusters
Black Holes
Black-Hole Hunters
Active Galaxies
Dark Matter and Dark Energy
Oddities of the Universe
Is there Anyone out there?
How Will it all End?

978 0 7502 9234 4